PAG

CYCLING

SHOOTING AND SHOWJUMPING

by Jason Page

HORSE POWER!

Cian O'Connor (IRL) on his way to winning gold on Waterford Crystal during the Mixed Individual Showjumping final, Athens 2004.

ANCIENT ORIGINS

This book covers very different events at the Olympics.
Some are all about strength. Others require great accuracy.

ANCIENT ORIGINS

Many of the modern Olympic events are actually
thousands of years old. For example, the ancient
Greeks held weightlifting
competitions using huge
heavy stones, while the first
sporting events involving horses
were chariot races. This Assyrian
carving of a chariot rider is more
than 2,500 years old.

Assyrian chariot

GAMES EVERYWHERE

The Olympic events in this book
will be held at a wide range of
venues in Beijing, from the
velodrome (cycle track) to
the shooting range hall,
and the archery field to the
equestrian venues. There
will even be a bicycle
motocross (bmx) venue.

SUPER STATS

Only 211 competitors took part
in the 1896 Olympics. When the
Games come to Beijing, more
than 10,500 athletes
will be hoping to
win a medal.

GOING FOR GOLD

At the ancient Olympic Games the winning competitors were awarded a simple crown made of olive branches. At the modern Olympics the winners are rewarded with medals made of solid gold.

Olympic commemorative medal, 1896

EXCELLENCE IN ACTION

Competitors with disabilities have excelled at power and precision events such as archery, shooting and horseriding. In 1952, Lis Hartel (DEN) became the first woman to win a medal in the dressage event, even though she was partially paralyzed and could not move her legs below the knee.

OLYMPICS FACT FILE

- The Olympic Games were first held in Olympia, in ancient Greece, around 3,000 years ago. They took place every four years until they were abolished in 393 CE.

- A Frenchman called Pierre de Coubertin (1863–1937) revived the Games, and the first modern Olympics were held in Athens in 1896.

- The modern Games have been held every four years since 1896, except in 1916, 1940 and 1944, due to war. Special 10th-anniversary Games took place in 1906.

- The symbol of the Olympic Games is five interlocking coloured rings. Together, they represent the five different continents from which athletes come to compete.

RACE AGAINST THE CLOCK

Each competitor has to fire a certain number
of arrows at the target within a set time.
In the individual events, the archers are given
40 seconds to fire each arrow; in the doubles
competitions, the firing time is reduced to
20 seconds per arrow.

Each
arrow must
have the archer's
initials engraved
on it.

This archer
is using a leather 'finger tab'
to pull back the bowstring.
Some archers prefer to wear
a glove instead.

DID YOU KNOW?

There were no Olympic
archery events
between 1924 and their
reintroduction in 1972.
They have been part of
the Games ever since.

The youngest person
to win an Olympic
medal in an archery
event was just 14 years
old; the oldest was 68!

If someone shouts
'Fast!' during a
competition, all the
competitors must stop
firing immediately.

A guard
made of plastic
or leather stops the
bow string injuring
the archer's arm
when it is
released.

Arrows
are kept in
a special bag
called a quiver
which is tied
around the
archer's
waist.

Archer

ARCHERY

People started using bows and arrows more than 25,000 years ago, which makes archery one of the oldest sports in the Games!

> The archer uses an adjustable sight (called a bowsight) to aim at the target.

IT'S A LONG SHOT!

Archery events were included in the Olympics for the first time in 1900. Over the years there have been many different archery events, including some that involved shooting moving targets. At the Games in Beijing all the archers will aim for fixed targets placed 70 metres away.

Olympic archery targets

> This stablizer balances the bow, helping the archer to hold it steady.

> A woman's bow must weigh more than 15 kg, while the bow used by men must weigh at least 22 kg.

ANIMAL OLYMPIANS

The appropriately named archerfish would be aiming for a gold medal at the Animal Olympics. It can shoot a drop of water from its mouth up to a metre away with incredible accuracy.

TAKE A BOW

Olympic archers use a bow known as a 'recurve' bow, which has ends that bend away from the archer. This type of bow was invented about 3,500 years ago.

ARCHERY (CONTINUED)

Archers need both physical and mental strength. Lifting the heavy bow and drawing back the tight bowstring requires strong muscles, while great powers of concentration are needed to focus on the target.

An archery target has five coloured circles. Each of these circles is divided into two halves by a thin line and is worth a different number of points. The closer an arrow is to the centre, the more points it scores.

SPORT FOR ALL

In 1984, Neroli Fairhall (NZL) made Olympic history when she took part in the women's archery event — she was the first athlete in a wheelchair ever to compete at the Olympic Games. Disabled athletes also have their own Games called the Paralympics, which will be held in Beijing two weeks after the Olympic Games.

Archery target

4 points

3 points

8 points

2 points

1 point

SUPER STATS

Once fired, arrows travel through the air at around 240 km/h — that's faster than the average speed of a Formula One racing car!

ITALIAN DEADEYE

At the Athens Olympics in 2004 Marco Galiazzo became the first Italian to win a gold medal in the men's individual archery. The 21-year-old beat Hiroshi Yamamoto (JPN) by two points, winning the match 111–109. Galiazzo said he had worked hard on his archery for four years to be his best. He also said it might take him another four years for him to realise he really had won a gold medal.

Bull's-eye: 10 points

9 points

5 points

6 points

7 points

Marco Galiazzo (ITA)

DID YOU KNOW

Another word for archery is toxophily.

Disabled athletes will compete in 18 different Olympic sports at the Paralympics in Beijing. It will be the thirteenth time these Games have been held.

If an arrow hits the line between two scoring bands on the target, the highest score is awarded.

TAKING AIM

The archery target measures 1.22 metres across — that's about the same height as an average eight-year-old. However, from where the archers are standing, the target looks the same size as a drawing pin held at arm's length!

Gunn-Rita Dahle (NOR)

RIDE ON!

Gunn-Rita Dahle, pictured left, is the frontrunner in the women's mountain bike event after winning the gold medal at the 2004 Olympics. Competition will be tough though, with number-one ranked rider in the world Irina Kalentieva (RUS) and Sabine Spitz (GER) picked as hot favourites.

Julien Absalon (FRA) is the current Olympic champion and a strong contender for a medal at the 2008 Games.

The handlebars on a mountain bike are usually straight. There's no bell but there are two powerful brakes!

DID YOU KNOW?

🦶 Mountain bikes have up to 24 gears and some bikes are also fitted with rear shock absorbers.

🦶 The first purpose-built mountain bike went on sale in 1981. Now, 70 percent of all bikes sold are mountain bikes!

🦶 Cyclists in the mountain bike events are not allowed to deliberately get in each other's way and must allow faster competitors to overtake them.

ON TRACK FOR VICTORY

The mountain bike events will be held on Beijing's Laoshan mountain along a 4.6 kilometre long course. Each lap will provide the competitors with a zigzagging and sloping track to challenge their skills and fitness. Usually the men race between 40 and 50 kilometres and the women 30 to 40 kilometres. The exact distance is decided the night before the race.

Mountain bikes are fitted with a fork-like front suspension to help absorb bumps and knocks.

The tyres on mountain bikes have deep treads to grip the slippery mud and are much wider than the tyres used in other cycling events.

MOUNTAIN BIKING

All cycling competitors must wear a helmet.

Mountain bike events are like cross-country running races — only on bikes! Mountain biking is a very new cycle sport and is only making its third appearance at the Games.

ANIMAL OLYMPIANS

When it comes to tackling tough terrain, the undisputed champion in the animal kingdom is a small goat-like antelope called the chamois. It can race up a rugged mountain, climbing up to 1,000 metres in just 15 minutes.

A mountain bike's frame is similar in design to a road or track bike but is made of stronger materials designed to withstand the tough terrain.

3

ATHENS 2004

Julien Absalon (FRA)

NO HELP AT ALL

Unlike other cycling sports, mountain bikers are not allowed to receive any help or assistance during the race. If their bike gets damaged, they have to repair it themselves.

Women's: Gunn-Rita Dahle (NOR)

CYCLING

For the road race and time trials, Olympic cyclists will take to Beijing's urban cycling track, which is surrounded by 24 new public parks and reforested land.

RIDING IN THE SLIPSTREAM

Cyclists in the road races usually ride together in tight packs so that they can use the rider in front of them as a windbreak. This means they don't have to pedal quite so hard to keep up! The technique, known as 'drafting', is forbidden in the time trial races.

Men's individual road race

SUPER STATS

The longest ever road race was held at the 1912 Games in Stockholm. It was 320 km long – that's like cycling from London to Paris!

TIME TRIAL

In the time trials, competitors start the race one at a time, with a gap of 90 seconds between each rider. The winner is the cyclist who completes the course in the fastest time, not the one who reaches the finish first. The men's event is 45.8 km long and the women's is 31.2 km.

ON YER BIKE!

The bikes used in road races are much lighter than mountain bikes and have much narrower tyres. The handlebars are curved, enabling riders to lean forwards in the saddle, reducing wind resistance and increasing their speed. Road race bikes have eight gears.

DID YOU KNOW?

)) Cyclists in the same national team are allowed to share food and swap tools during the road race!

)) In both the road race and the time trials, support vehicles may follow the riders and help carry out any emergency repairs to their bikes.

)) At the 1896 Olympics the road race was won by a Greek rider who borrowed a bike from a spectator after crashing his own!

The reigning women's time trials champion is Leontien Zijlaard-van Moorsel (NED).

Leontien Zijlaard-van Moorsel (NED)

ROAD RACE

The road races are straightforward — but very long! All the competitors start at the same time and the winner is the first to cross the finish line. Each lap of the course is 18 km. Men complete 13 laps (234 km) and women complete 7 laps (126 km).

Women's road race: Sara Carrigan (AUS) **Women's time trial:** Leontien Zijlaard-van Moorsel (NED)

Velodrome, 1996 Olympics

DROME FROM DROME

All the track events are held inside a purpose-built cycling track called a velodrome. The surface of the velodrome is made of wood and slopes so that the outside of the track is much higher than the inside. One lap of the velodrome is 250 metres.

Chris Boardman (GBR) won the men's individual pursuit at the 1992 Games on this bike which weighed just 8 kg.

DID YOU KNOW?

Cycling is one of only five sports that have been included in every modern Olympic Games. The others are fencing, gymnastics, athletics and swimming.

Cycling and canoeing are the only Olympic events that are timed to 1,000th of a second!

The velodrome used in the 1964 Olympics in Tokyo cost around £500,000 to build. It was only used for four days and then knocked down!

The seat on Boardman's bike was higher than the handlebars.

To help reduce drag, the back wheel on most track bikes is solid (it's known as a disc wheel), while the front wheel usually has just three spokes.

CYCLING (CONTINUED)

There are 12 'track' events for cyclists – four for women and eight for men.

Track riders wear aerodynamic helmets designed to reduce wind-resistance (known as 'drag') and help them travel faster.

NAME THAT RACE

Individual pursuit – two riders start on opposite sides of the track with the aim of catching their opponent. If, after 16 laps (12 laps in the women's event), neither rider has been caught, the cyclist who crosses their own finish line first is the winner.

Team pursuit – similar to the individual pursuit except that this race is contested by two teams of four riders each. Only men compete in this event.

Points race – competitors race for 160 laps (100 laps in the women's event). At the end of every tenth lap they are awarded points according to their position: five for first, three for second, two for third and one for fourth. The winner is the rider with the most points.

Madison – a team version of the points race, for men only, which takes place over 240 laps. The two-man teams are usually made up of a sprinter and a long-distance cyclist who take it in turns to race against the opposing team.

SUPER STATS

France has won 82 medals in the Olympic cycling events, including 39 golds – that's more than any other nation! In second place with 58 medals is Italy, while Great Britain is third with 46.

Women's points race: Olga Slyusareva (RUS)
Women's individual pursuit: Sarah Ulmer (NZL)

CYCLING
(CONTINUED)

The remaining track events are all time trials or sprints. Time trials focus on speed, while sprints test riders' cunning as well as their strength.

BATTLE OF WITS

Sprinters, such as Olympic champion Jens Fielder (GER), use cunning tactics to win. The riders usually begin very slowly and may even stop on the second lap in an attempt to get into the best position for the sudden race to the finish.

ANIMAL OLYMPIANS

Jens Fielder achieved a record speed of over 70 km/h during the 1992 Olympics but that's nothing compared to the top speed of a sprinting cheetah. These super-speedy big cats can race along at around 100 km/h.

Jens Fielder (GER)

NAME THAT RACE

Time trial – cyclists race against the clock and the rider with the fastest time wins. The men's race is four laps and the women's race is two laps.

Sprint – a three-lap race between two riders. However, the riders spend the first two laps jockeying for position before making a final dash over the last 200 metres to the finish line.

Olympic sprint – two three-man teams race against each other over three laps and the fastest team wins. Only men compete in this event.

Keirin – for men only, this is an eight-lap race but competitors remain behind a motorbike for the first 5.5 laps. The motorbike gradually speeds up from 25 km/h to 40 km/h before leaving the track and allowing the cyclists to sprint to the finish.

NO BRAKES!

The bikes used in track events don't have any brakes! They also have just one gear. This means that cyclists must pedal all the time to keep moving.

The reigning time trials Olympic champion Chris Hoy (GBR) holds up the gold medal he won at the 2004 games.

DID YOU KNOW?

The 1896 Olympics included a 12-hour track race. Only three contestants managed to finish the event and it was never held again!

Until 1972, there was a cycling event for tandems – bicycles ridden by two people.

During the semi-final of the men's sprint in 1964, both riders stood still for more than 21 minutes, waiting for the other to make his move!

Women's sprint: Lori-Ann Muenzer (CAN)
Women's 500-metres time trial: Anna Meares (AUS)

DID YOU KNOW?

〽 In 1956, when the Olympics were last held in Australia, all the equestrian events took place in Sweden. This was because Australia's strict quarantine laws wouldn't allow competitors' horses into the country!

〽 In 1932, the course was so difficult that no team managed to complete it – and no medals were awarded!

〽 In the event of a tie, the course is rearranged and the competitors are timed as they go around again.
This is called a 'jump off'.
If they end up with the same score again, the rider with the best time wins.

EQUAL OPPORTUNITIES

Equestrian sports do not have separate events for men and women. All the competitions are open to riders (and horses!) of both sexes. As well as the individual event, there is also a team event in which four riders from the same country compete together.

Upright

The showjumping arena is 120 metres long and 80 metres wide. That's slightly longer and wider than a football pitch.

Showjumping arena

A FAULTLESS PERFORMANCE

In 1992, Ludger Beerbaum (GER) became only the fourth competitor in the history of the Games to win the gold after picking up no penalty points at all.

Ludger Beerbaum (GER)

REIGNING OLYMPIC CHAMPIONS: Individual jumping: Rodrigo Pessoa (on Baloubet du Rouet) (BRA)

SHOWJUMPING

There are three different horse riding competitions (or 'equestrian' events as they are known) at the Olympics. So saddle up and get ready to gallop into number one – showjumping!

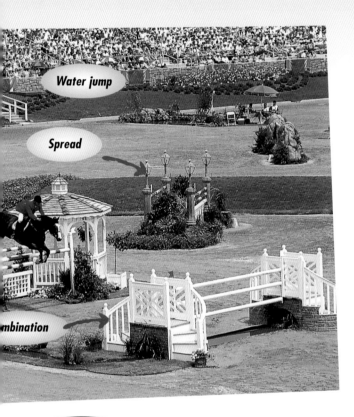

Water jump

Spread

mbination

IT'S ALL YOUR FAULT

In showjumping, horse and rider have to go around a course which contains at least 15 jumps. The idea is to clear all the jumps in the right order within the required time limit, picking up as few penalty points as possible. These penalties are called 'faults' and they are awarded for a range of different mistakes, for example when the horse knocks down fences or refuses to jump.

LEARN THE LINGO

Courses are constructed using four basic types of jump.

Uprights – these are the tallest jumps and may be up to 1.7 metres high.

Spreads – these are wider than uprights but also lower.

Combinations – these are made up of two or three jumps placed a few strides apart.

Water jumps – these are shallow water-filled troughs which may be up to 4.5 metres wide.

DRESSAGE

The word 'dressage' comes from a French word meaning 'training' and this event is all about testing the riders' control of their horses.

DOING THE ROUNDS

The individual competition consists of three rounds. In the first two, competitors must perform a set routine of moves and manoeuvres. However, the third is a freestyle round, which gives the riders a chance to show off their skills by performing their own routines set to music.

ANIMAL OLYMPIANS

The most successful horse in the history of the Games was called Rembrandt. Between 1988 and 1992, it won no less than four gold medals in the dressage events!

SOLDIER ON

Until 1952, only commissioned officers in the armed forces were allowed to compete in the Olympic dressage events. This rule was applied very strictly. When it was discovered that one member of the winning Swedish team in 1948 had a lower rank, the team was disqualified.

MAKING YOUR POINT

Each dressage competition is scored by five judges who sit in different positions around the arena. They award the horse and rider points out of 10 for each move. Basic dressage moves include the pirouette (a tight turn in which the horse keeps one of its back legs in the same spot), the passage (a very slow, elegant trot) and the piaffer (trotting on the spot).

Isabell Werth (GER)

DID YOU KNOW?

Lorna Johnstone (GBR) became the oldest woman to compete in the Olympics when she took part in the dressage in 1972, five days after her 70th birthday!

Riders are forbidden to communicate with their horse by making noises.

Contestants can lose points if their horse swishes its tail or puts its ears back!

LOOK SMART

As you can see from this picture of 1996 gold medallist, Isabell Werth (GER), competitors in dressage events must follow a strict dress code. This includes top hat and tails, a white shirt, polished black boots and white breeches. Riders who work in the police or armed forces are allowed to wear their uniforms.

Team dressage: GERMANY

DID YOU KNOW?

🐎 In 1936, one competitor fell off his horse during the cross-country run and took almost 3 hours to catch it again. He ended up with over 18,000 penalty points!

🐎 In the event of a draw at the end of the three-day event, the team or rider with the best cross-country score is the winner.

🐎 Riders must use the same horse in all three parts of the three-day event.

BIG BREAKS

Three-day eventing is by far the toughest of the equestrian events — as the medical reports prove! At least four Olympic gold medallists have stood on the winners' podium with broken bones. They include Wendy Schaeffer, a member of the victorious Australian team at the 1996 Olympics. When asked about her injury, Schaeffer replied: "It's nothing drastic, just a broken leg!"

BUSY DAYS

The individual competition is spread over three days, while the team event takes four days. There are four riders in each team. On day one (and day two in the team event), competitors take part in the dressage competition. This is followed by a speed and endurance day, and showjumping on the final day.

Leslie Law (on Shear L'Eau) (GBR)

THREE-DAY EVENT

The three-day event combines dressage and showjumping with a gruelling cross-country ride. It's the ultimate challenge for horse and rider and tests their skill and stamina to the limits.

CROSS-COUNTRY

The cross-country ride forms the final part of what's called the 'speed and endurance day'. The aim is to avoid penalty points by jumping the obstacles and finishing within the required time. The day consists of four 'phases':

A. Flat roads and tracks: 4.4 km

B. Steeplechase in which the horses must jump nine fences: 3.105 km

C. Flat roads and tracks: 7.92 km

D. Cross-county, with up to 35 obstacles: 7.41 km.

Mark Todd (NZL) won four Olympic medals in the three-day event between 1984 and 1992.

Mark Todd

SUPER STATS

German competitors have dominated the equestrian events, winning over 34 gold medals. At the 1936 Olympics they produced the one-and-only 'clean sweep' – winning gold in all six events. Switzerland has won 17 golds and France has won 12.

Leslie Law (GBR)

SHOOTING: PISTOL

Are you ready? Then get very steady to take a look at the pistol shooting competitions. In these events, the slightest wobble can cost you a gold medal!

QUICK-FIRE ROUNDS

In the men's rapid fire event, competitors have only a short time to take aim and shoot. In the first round, they are allowed 8 seconds to fire five shots at five different targets. The time limit is reduced to 6 seconds in the second round and 4 seconds in the final round.

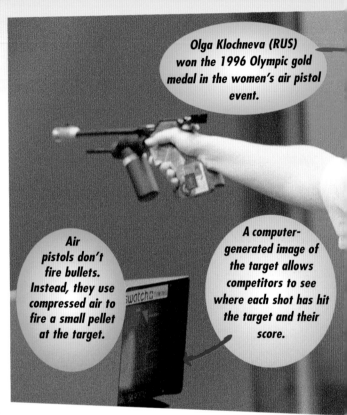

Olga Klochneva (RUS) won the 1996 Olympic gold medal in the women's air pistol event.

Air pistols don't fire bullets. Instead, they use compressed air to fire a small pellet at the target.

A computer-generated image of the target allows competitors to see where each shot has hit the target and their score.

ANIMAL OLYMPIANS

The sharp shooting star of the animal kingdom is the spitting cobra. When threatened, the snake shoots poisonous venom out of its mouth with deadly accuracy. It always aims for its enemy's eyes and can score a direct hit at a range of more than 2 metres!

REIGNING OLYMPIC CHAMPIONS: MEN: Air pistol: Wang Yifu (CHN) / **Free pistol:** Mikhail Nestruev (RUS) / **Rapid fire pistol:** Ralf Schumann (GER)

Károly Takács was a member of Hungary's world-champion pistol-shooting team when in 1938 his right hand was blown off by a grenade during an army training exercise. However, Takács was determined that it wouldn't be the end of his shooting career. He spent 10 years teaching himself to shoot left-handed and went on to win two Olympic gold medals!

Ear protectors block out any distracting sounds and help competitors to concentrate.

Competitors wear blinkers around their eyes to help them focus on the target.

DID YOU KNOW?

Pierre de Coubertin, the founder of the modern Olympic Games, was a former French pistol-shooting champion.

Women competed in the shooting events for the first time in 1968. Women-only events were introduced in 1984.

Pistol shooters must hold the gun with one hand only.

Olga Klochneva (RUS)

ON TARGET

The distance of the target depends on the event. In air pistol competitions, it's 10 metres away; in the rapid fire and sports pistol events, it's 25 metres away; and in the free pistol, it's 50 metres away. Each target consists of 10 rings; each ring is worth a different score, from 1–10 points.

Rapid fire targets

Men's rifle competition (prone)

When shooting outside, blinkers also shield the competitor's eyes from changes in the light.

TAKING UP POSITION

In the air rifle and running target events competitors stand up to shoot. In the 'prone' event they shoot lying down on the ground, while in the 'three position' event they fire from standing, kneeling and lying positions. Whatever the position, the competitors are forbidden to let their rifles touch or rest against any other object.

DID YOU KNOW?

In 1920, 72-year-old Oscar Swahn (SWE) became the oldest Olympic medallist in any sport when he won silver in one of the rifle events.

To a marksman, the bull's-eye on the shooting target looks as big as a full stop.

The most successful marksman in the history of the Games was Carl Osburn (USA) who won 11 medals (five gold, four silver and two bronze) between 1912 and 1924.

Marksmen are not allowed to wear clothing with straps, laces or seams.

BULL'S-EYE

At the Games in 1956, Gerald Ouellette (CAN) scored 600 points in the prone event — the highest possible score! However, his score never received official recognition because the rifle range turned out to be 1.5 metres too short. The first official perfect score of 600 was eventually achieved in the prone event by Miroslav Varaga (TCH) in 1988.

SHOOTING: RIFLE

Six different events involve shooting with rifles — two are for women and four are for men.

This black square blocks out the vision from the eye the competitor isn't using.

MOVING TARGET

In the running target event, competitors have to shoot a moving target as it slides across a gap between two protective walls. The target moves at two speeds — on a slow run the competitors have 5 seconds to shoot; on a fast run, they have just 2.5 seconds! This is the only event in which competitors are allowed to aim using a telescopic sight.

Yuri Fedkine (EUN)

Marksmen usually wear a glove on the hand that holds the rifle but not on the hand that pulls the trigger.

Yuri Fedkine (EUN) won the men's air rifle event at the 1992 Games.

SUPER STATS

The USA has shot to the top of the winners' table in the shooting events, with 46 gold medals. In second place is Russia (former Soviet Union) with 29 golds, while Norway is third with 16 wins.

SHOOTING: SHOT GUN

At the 1900 Olympics people shot at real pigeons. Fortunately, the only pigeons people will be shooting at the Olympic games in Beijing will be clay ones.

WATCH THE BIRDIE!

Competitors in the Olympic shot gun events shoot at saucer-shaped targets known as 'clay pigeons', or 'clays' for short. Clays are catapulted through the air at great speed by a device called a trap. The aim is to shoot the clays before they go out of range or hit the ground.

READY, AIM, FIRE!

At Beijing both men and women will compete in three different types of shot gun events:

1. **Trap:** the clays are released one at a time and contestants get two shots at each one.

2. **Double trap:** two clays are released at the same time and contestants get only one shot at each one.

3. **Skeet:** contestants move around shooting from eight different positions or 'stations' on the course. The clays are released two at a time and competitors are allowed one shot at each.

GUNS WITHOUT BULLETS

The guns used in other Olympic shooting events fire a single bullet or pellet, but a shot gun fires lots of little round balls called 'shot'. As these balls fly through the air, they start to spread out, covering a much wider area than just one bullet. This is why shot guns are used to hit difficult, fast-moving targets at close range.

Double trap: Kim Rhode (USA)

DID YOU KNOW?

- Clay pigeons aren't made of clay at all, but from a mixture of limestone and tar.

- Clays fly out of the traps at 85 km/h – as fast as a real pigeon can fly at top speed!

- In trap and double trap events, the clay is released as soon as the competitor shouts 'pull!'. In skeet events, there can be a delay of up to 3 seconds.

Ennio Falco (ITA)

Ennio Falco (ITA) celebrates his victory in the skeet competition at the 1996 Games. To be a champion in the shot gun events requires lightning reactions as well as super accuracy.

LEARN THE LINGO

Birds – another word for clays

Pull! – competitors shout out 'pull' when they are ready to shoot

Trap – a machine that launches the clays into the air

Choke – this part of the gun determines how wide the shot spreads

Cartridge – shot gun ammunition

DID YOU KNOW?

⁇ Many changes took place in weightlifting at the 2000 Games — the number of weight categories was reduced from 10 to 8 and women's events were contested for the first time.

⁇ Ancient Egyptian wall paintings from 4,000 years ago show weightlifters using bags filled with sand.

⁇ At the 1896 Olympic Games there was a weightlifting event which only allowed the use of one arm!

Naim Suleymanoglu (TUR)

THE SNATCH

In the snatch, competitors must lift the weight above their head in one single movement. As they hoist the weight above them, they squat down underneath it and lock their arms. Then, keeping the weight at arm's length above their head, they stand up straight. Here, three-time Olympic champion Naim Suleymanoglu (TUR) shows how it's done.

THE CLEAN & JERK

In the clean and jerk event, competitors lift the weight above their head in two stages. First they raise the bar onto their chests — this must be done in a single, 'clean' movement. Then they thrust the bar over their heads with a quick 'jerk' movement and stand up straight.

MEN'S WEIGHTLIFTING

*T*he mighty weightlifters are the strongest competitors at the Olympic Games.

WEIGHT FOR IT!

Weightlifters at the Olympics compete in different weight classes according to how heavy they are. However, the rules in each event are the same. All competitors must perform two different sorts of lift — called the 'snatch' and the 'clean and jerk'. The heaviest weight they manage to lift in the first category is added to the heaviest one in the second category to give their final score. And whoever has the highest total is the winner!

SUPER STATS

The strongest weightlifters can lift three times their own bodyweight using the clean and jerk technique!

HOLD EVERYTHING!

Competitors are allowed three attempts at each lift. They are watched by three judges who decide whether the attempt is successful. A valid lift is when the weight is held above the head with the arms out straight. The feet must be in a straight line and contestants must be standing still. Sometimes the weight is just too heavy — the legs buckle and down go the weight *and* the competitor, as happened here to Manfred Norlinger (GER)!

Manfred Norlinger (GER)

85 kg: George Asanidze (GEO) 94 kg: Milen Dobrev (BUL) 105 kg: Dmitry Berestov (RUS) 105 kg-plus: Hossein Reza Zadeh (IRI)

WOMEN'S WEIGHTLIFTING

At the 2000 Games women were able to compete in the weightlifting for the first time in Olympic history.

ANIMAL OLYMPIANS

When it comes to weightlifting, ants are in a league of their own. Despite their small size, these tiny insects can lift and carry things 50 times their own bodyweight. If humans could do the same, heavyweight weightlifters would be able to pick up more than 5 tonnes with ease — that's as heavy as five family cars!

POWDER UP

The part of the bar which the competitors hold has a rough, bevelled surface to stop it slipping in their hands. Weightlifters are also allowed to put chalk dust on their hands to improve their grip.

COLOUR CODE

The different weights used in weightlifting are colour-coded. But don't forget, when working out how much a competitor is lifting, to add on 15 kg (20 kg in the men's event) for the bar and 5 kg for the two collars which hold the weights in place.

RED — 25 kg	**BLUE** — 20 kg
YELLOW — 15 kg	**GREEN** — 10 kg
WHITE — 5 kg	**BLACK** — 2.5 kg

Xia Yang (CHN)

THAT'S THE WAY TO DO IT!

Each weightlifter must hold the weight above her head until the judges are satisfied that she has it under control and that her feet are in a line. The referee will then give a signal indicating that she may put the weight down. Competitors must lower the bar to waist level before releasing their grip and letting go.

GREAT EXPECTATIONS

In the short time women have been allowed to compete at Olympic weightlifting, China has come top of the table. Chinese athletes won seven gold medals at both the Sydney and the Athens games, and will be the team to look out for at Beijing.

DID YOU KNOW?

At the Games in 1924 one competitor in the weightlifting event was only 13 years old!

The weightlifter Harold Sakata (USA), a silver medallist at the 1948 Olympics, went on to star as Oddjob in the James Bond film Goldfinger.

After each successful lift the weight on the bar must be increased by at least 2.5 kg, unless the competitor is attempting to break the world record.

INDEX

Acknowledgements

We would like to thank Ian Hodge, Rosalind Beckman and Elizabeth Wiggans for their assistance.
Cartoons by John Alston.
Copyright © 2000 ticktock Entertainment Ltd.
Revised edition 2008 ticktock Media Ltd., 2 Orchard Business Centre, North Farm Road, Tunbridge Wells, TN2 3XF, UK.
All rights reserved. No part of this publication may be reproduced, stored in a retrieval system, or transmitted in any form or by any means electronic, mechanical, photocopying, recording or otherwise, without prior written permission of the copyright owner.
A CIP catalogue record for this book is available from the British Library.
ISBN 978 1 84696 733 7

Picture Credits: t = top, b = bottom, l = left, r = right, OFC = outside front cover,
OBC = outside back cover, IFC = inside front cover

Allsport; IFC, 3tr, 4/5 (main pic), 5tr, 6/7c, 10/11 (main pic), 12tl, 12/13 (main pic), 14/15 (main pic),
16/17 (main pic), 16br, 18/19 (main pic), 19tr, 21r, 22/23c, 23br, 24tl, 24/25 (main pic), 26/27 (main pic), 26t,
28/29b, 30/31 (main pic), 30/31c. Steve Bardens/ Action Plus: OFC. Adam Davy/ Empics Sport/ PA Photos: 8t. Image select: 2/3c. Robert Laberge/ Getty
Images: 7tr. Phil Noble/ PA Archive/ PA Photos: 15b. Reuters/ Mike Finn-Kelcey: 20. Sipa Press/ Rex Features: 9l, 11b. Michael Steele/ EMPICS Sport/ PA
Photos: 28t.

Picture research by Image Select. Printed in China.